SPORTS
I SPY BOOK

I spy with my little eye a sport starting with...

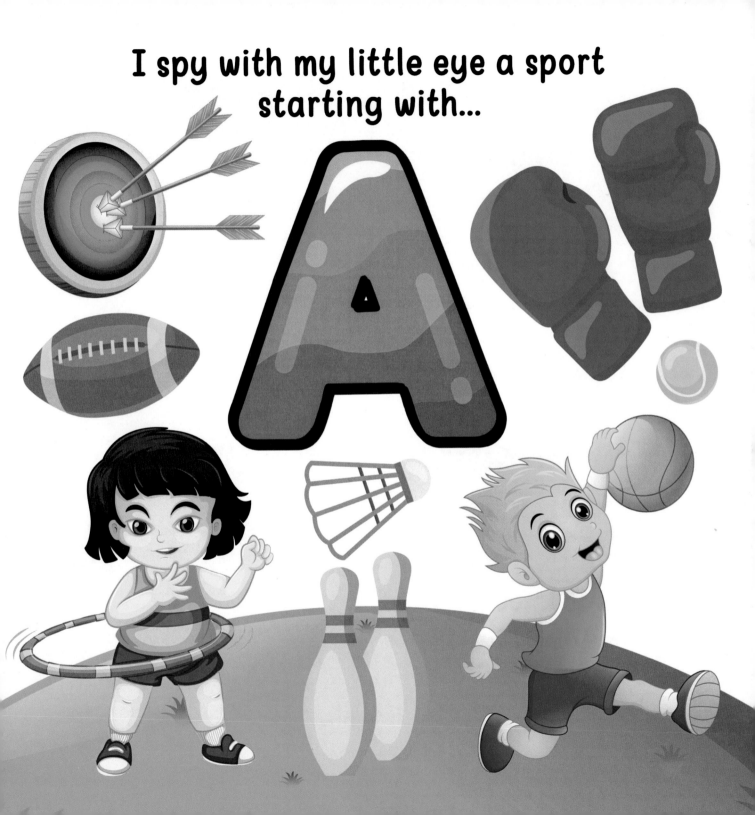

DID YOU KNOW?
The first known use of bows and arrows was by the Babylonians.

A
is for Archery

I spy with my little eye a sport starting with...

B

B is for Baseball

DID YOU KNOW?

There are 9 innings in baseball.

I spy with my little eye a sport starting with...

 **is for Cricket**

DID YOU KNOW?
The first cricket ball was made of wool.

I spy with my little eye a sport starting with...

D

DID YOU KNOW?
Jacques Cousteau invented scuba diving equipment.

D is for Diving

I spy with my little eye a sport starting with...

E

I spy with my little eye a sport starting with...

F is for Football

DID YOU KNOW?
Football was invented in 1882.

I spy with my little eye a sport starting with...

DID YOU KNOW? Golf was invented in Scotland.

G is for Golf

I spy with my little eye a sport starting with...

 **is for Hockey**

DID YOU KNOW?
The roots of hockey were from Egypt.

I spy with my little eye a sport starting with...

I is for Ice Dancing

DID YOU KNOW?
Ballet on ice is a type of ice dancing.

I spy with my little eye a sport starting with...

K

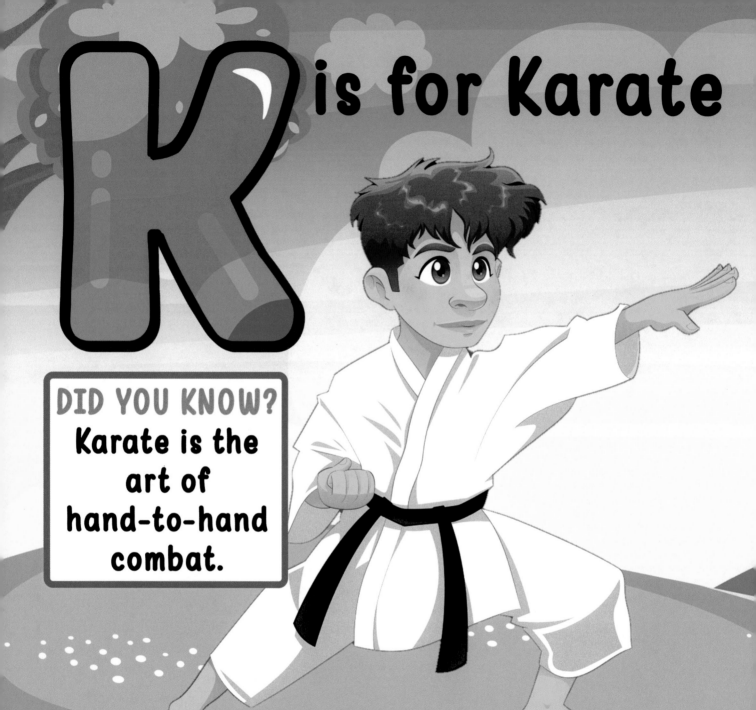

K is for Karate

DID YOU KNOW?
Karate is the art of hand-to-hand combat.

I spy with my little eye a sport starting with...

L is for Long Jump

I spy with my little eye a sport starting with...

M

is for Marathon

DID YOU KNOW?
The marathon's race is usually
26 miles and 385 yards.

I spy with my little eye a sport starting with...

N is for Netball

DID YOU KNOW?
The marathon's race is usually 26 miles and 385 yards.

I spy with my little eye a sport starting with...

O AND P

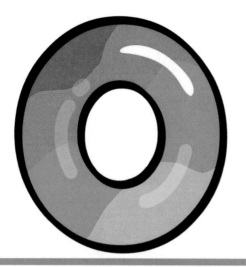 **is for Olympics**

DID YOU KNOW?
Summer and Winter Olympics are held every two years.

DID YOU KNOW?
Ping Pong's other name is table tennis.

is for Ping Pong

I spy with my little eye a sport starting with...

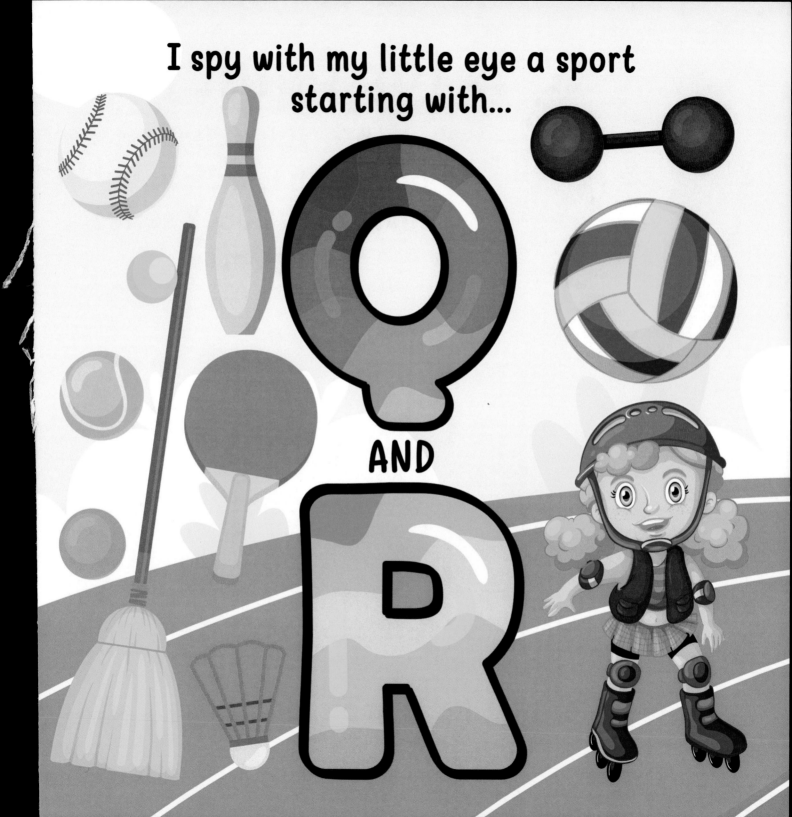

is for Quidditch

DID YOU KNOW?
Quidditch is a fictional sport in the book series Harry Potter.

R is for Roller Skating

DID YOU KNOW?
Roller skating is good for your heart.

I spy with my little eye a sport starting with...

DID YOU KNOW?
Before yellow tennis balls, they were white.

is for Tennis

DID YOU KNOW?
Swimming burns lots of calories.

is for Swimming

I spy with my little eye a sport starting with...

AND

V

is for Volleyball

U

is for Underwater Sports

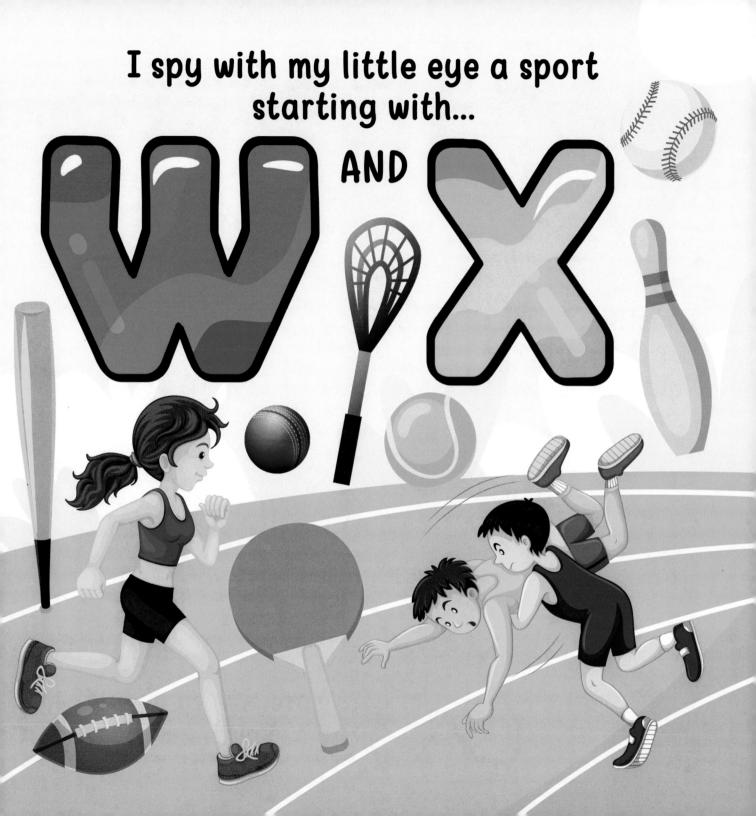

W is for Wrestling

X is for Xare

I spy with my little eye a sport starting with...

AND

Z

is for Zipline

is for Yacht Racing

Y

Made in the USA
Monee, IL
03 September 2022

13209932R00026